simply living smart

EVERYDAY SOLUTIONS FOR A
MORE ORGANIZED YOU!

simply living smart

- EVERYDAY SOLUTIONS FOR A
- MORE ORGANIZED YOU!

●● ● anitra kerr

Cofounder of simplylivingsmart.com

Bonneville Books
Springville, Utah

ISBN 13: 978-1-59955-207-1

Published by Bonneville Books, an imprint of Cedar Fort, Inc., 2373 W. 700 S., Springville, UT 84663
Distributed by Cedar Fort, Inc., www.cedarfort.com

  Library of Congress Cataloging-in-Publication Data

Kerr, Anitra, 1971-
  Simply living smart : everyday solutions for a more organized you / Anitra Kerr.
    p. cm.
  ISBN 978-1-59955-207-1
  1. Parents--Life skills guides. 2. Life skills. 3. Time management. 4. Organization. 5. Home economics. 6. Family--Time management. I. Title.

  HQ755.8.K48 2008
  640--dc22
                                2008028164

Cover design by Angela Olsen
Cover design © 2008 by Lyle Mortimer
Edited and typeset by Allison M. Kartchner

Printed in the United States of America

10 9 8 7 6 5 4 3 2 1

Printed on acid-free paper

Dedication

To my sweet husband, Erik, for convincing me that my 3 AM pillow talks should be written in a book, and to my four sons, Gabe, Christian, Ethan, and Hayden, who have been a part of all of my experiments in trying to achieve balance in the home.

Contents

Preface

Life is wonderful, isn't it? Each day offers us the opportunity for new growth, a chance to rediscover who we are, and ways to learn how life can be better! We all have our challenges, commitments, and schedules, but let us not forget that we as women are also individuals: souls who need nurturing and scheduled "time-outs"! As a wife and a mother of four boys, I have come to appreciate three important words—delegation, organization, and relaxation. Each one has its place in the home, and if practiced regularly, can create harmony and a feeling of well-being.

Nothing is more stressful to me than a home of chaos—a place where disorder, bad manners, or disharmony rules. Of course, we all have our days when we feel that this is our plight, but have no fear—it can be changed.

Learning to delegate responsibilities in the home can alleviate a lot of stress generally placed on a mother. You are helping those in your household to learn responsibility and commitment to the family as you teach them to contribute to household chores. They learn the joy of serving others while acquiring skills that will benefit them in the future. I believe that the skills learned in the home are invaluable.

Over the years, through study and coaching, I have discovered tips and tricks that have helped me to live a more balanced and organized life, to find joy in the moment, and to look forward to each day. This is why I'm excited to share this book with you, in hopes of inspiring you to look beyond the repetition of your everyday affairs and enjoy the sometimes mundane tasks that are set before you. Developing habits of organization will help you feel confident in running your home. Having an organized pantry, for example, can make your meal planning simple and enjoyable; creating a mini home office can keep you abreast of all your paperwork; and learning how to involve your family in household chores can create feelings of unity, as all work together to achieve harmony and order in the home.

I have broken down my organizing system into the seven days of the week, setting apart one day of the week for a pampering "time-out." My theory is that if my cup isn't full, there's little to give when others need me. While I have included many ideas for home organization, it is not my intent to intimidate you or make you believe that all of these activities need to be done every week. My suggestion is to pick those ideas that appeal to you, and perhaps work on one or two a week, until you have mastered the skill of organization in that area. It may take months to incorporate all of these ideas, but as you begin to practice these skills, you will appreciate the peace of mind that comes with living a more organized life. You'll free up more time for yourself and the ones you love, and you will feel the weight of everyday life lifted because of your new habits.

You'll become better at meal planning, budgeting, organizing, filing, cleaning, and much more. You'll appreciate time with friends and time alone just recharging and relaxing.

Learning to prioritize your activities begins with determining who is most important in your life, and what kind of time you'd like to invest in those things or people. If the interest of your family is truly supreme, schedule their needs first. Consider the time spent saying "yes" to everyone else who asks you to "just do me a favor," and ask yourself if you could not be replaced by someone else once in a while. Learn to kindly say "no." I have observed that simply saying "I'm sorry, I have another commitment," works like a charm. The person asking the favor doesn't need to know whether your "other commitment" is time with yourself, time at the doctor's, or what have you. Don't be afraid to say no. Your calendar will not suffer if it's not filled up every day. Allow yourself some breathing room.

Remember, you are only one person, but your influence can be great! You will feel empowered with your newly found skills and will love sharing what you've learned with your friends and family. As a woman, you set the tone for an environment conducive to joy and well-being in your home. As you teach the ones you love to do their part in contributing to the affairs of the home, everyone benefits. Now, take a deep breath, because you are on your way to simply living smart—every day!

Chapter One

Savoring Sundays

"Mid pleasures and palaces though we may roam,
Be it ever so humble, there's no place like home."
—*John Howard Payne*

I cherish Sundays. To me they symbolize newness—a time to recharge, to recommit, and to focus on my own little family. It's a time to reconnect and look forward to a new week! Since I don't like spending my Sundays cooking, cleaning, or doing dishes, I don't schedule any dinner parties at my home on that day. Just a quiet, simple meal with my own family and time for laughter and great conversation with my husband and my children. We love to take long afternoon naps, play board games, and bake delicious treats. We enjoy a simple candlelight dinner at the end of the day and we talk about everyone's plans for the week. I bring the calendar to the table, and we make sure that everything is well arranged and scheduled to ensure that our week runs smoothly.

One of my favorite times of the day is naptime. We take the phone off the hook, and all is quiet for a time. My family usually sleeps longer than I do, so I take advantage of the quiet to plan my menus for the week. My system is simple and refreshing! I'd like to share it with you.

Simple Meal-Planning

Did you know that most American families eat the same ten meals over and over again? To me this is simply inconceivable—we all need more variety than that! Imagine how nice it would be to have a variety of ninety to one hundred meals, with no extra hassle! It's not only possible, it's rewarding. Your family will actually look forward to dinner, and you will love the ooh's and aah's that come from pulling off something new every night!

You can begin by writing down your family's ten favorite meals and then making a list of the ingredients needed for those meals. As you think of more menu ideas, simply add them to your list. For example, spaghetti and meatballs with a fresh salad, or clam chowder and cornbread. Once you've made a list of all the ingredients needed to prepare those meals, take a look inside your pantry. Do you have all of the dry or canned ingredients available to repeat those same recipes, perhaps four or five times? If not, make those ingredients a priority, and as you go to the store, begin to stock up on those items that you most commonly use. In chapter 3, I'll share some great shopping tricks that will teach you how to shop smart and save on your grocery bills. I believe that to prepare well-balanced meals full of valuable nutrition, it's important to learn how to shop for fresh foods regularly, as well as learn to keep a well-stocked pantry.

Menu-Planning Calendar

Once you've determined your ten or twenty favorite meals, write them each on a 1x1-inch sticky note and stick it up on your wall calendar—one dinner idea for each of the next ten to twenty days. Include side dishes and perhaps a simple dessert. I even go as far as to color code my sticky notes—blue for pasta, green for beans, pink for meat, yellow for salads, and purple for soups. This way, I'm sure to mix up my menus in a more balanced way, so that I don't serve chicken, for example, twice in a row. Once I've served one of these meals, and it's been a success, I simply take the sticky note and place it on a calendar date two months down the line. This way, if I know the dinner was a success, I can repeat it without having to reinvent another meal. If it wasn't so popular, I simply throw away the sticky note, and move on. As you add more favorites, your calendar will soon be filled with exciting dishes that your family loves. Before long, you will have ninety to one hundred different meals your family loves to eat. And because you'll keep rotating your menu papers to future weeks, you'll know in March what your family will be eating in June! Can you see how time-saving this exercise can be?

One way to save time in meal planning is to make a list of those meals that your family particularly likes. That can be done by listing the name or description of the meal at the top of the page, and below each one, jotting down the ingredients. That way you will know immediately what you need for meal preparation. The following is an example of what that list might look like. You can simply adjust it to your own needs and desires.

Dinner Ideas

Spaghetti and Meatballs	Chicken Enchiladas	Split Pea Soup
spaghetti	flour tortillas	split peas
ground beef	shredded chicken	chicken bouillon
bread crumbs	mozzarella cheese	potatoes
egg	mild chilies	carrots
onions	crm. of chikn. soup	celery
spaghetti sauce	milk	cream cheese
salt and pepper	onions	

Kids' Lunches and Snacks

Are you ever at a loss when trying to keep a little variety in your kids' lunches or after-school snacks? Do you sometimes worry about the nutritional benefits of some of the snacks children might prefer? How can we help them choose more wisely? Sometimes all it takes is making the snacks fun by preparing them with a flare: like oatmeal-raisin cookies on a stick, animal crackers arranged on a plate beneath celery-stick trees, low-sugar fruit leather, and dried fruit in little plastic bags.

Here are a couple of examples of varying the presentation of snacks with a little pizzazz.

Kid-Friendly "Sushi" Rolls

· ·

1 slice whole-grain bread
1 banana
1 Tbsp. raisins
2 Tbsp. peanut or almond butter

With a rolling pin flatten the slice of bread until thin, like a tortilla.
Spread the bread with peanut butter and sprinkle with raisins.
Lay the whole banana on one edge of the bread and roll it up tightly into a roll.
Turn the roll with the long edge facing down. With a sharp knife, cut the roll into 1-inch slices.
Enjoy!

Oatmeal Cookies on Parade

· ·

20 pretzel rods, cut into 4-inch lengths
½ cup crushed peanuts or walnuts
½ tsp. salt

2 sticks butter
1 cup granulated sugar
2 eggs
1 tsp. vanilla
1 tsp. baking powder
1 tsp. baking soda
2½ cups all purpose flour
2½ cups rolled oats or multi-grain rolled cereal
1 cup raisins or chocolate chips

Make cookie dough by blending the butter, salt, and sugar until smooth, then mixing in the eggs and vanilla until consistent. Blend the baking powder and baking soda into the flour and beat into the egg mixture. Fold in the rolled oats and raisins (or chocolate chips) until well mixed.

Roll the dough into dough balls, and press them into the crushed walnuts or peanuts.

Lay 8 pretzel rods on a lightly greased cookie sheet. Place a cookie-dough ball on the end of each pretzel rod, flattening gently to resemble a lollipop. Bake at 350°F for 8–10 min. Allow to cool completely.

Edible Animal Friends

Animal crackers
½ cup cream cheese
3 Tbsp. peanut butter, separated
1 tsp. powdered sugar (optional)
Celery stalks cut into 4-inch lengths (preferably with the leafy part still attached)
Apple rings

Slice an apple into rings about ¼-inch thick and press one or two rings flat against each serving plate. In a small bowl combine 2 tablespoons peanut butter, cream cheese, and powdered sugar until creamy. Spread mixture inside the groove of each celery stick.

Cut a small slit in one side of each apple ring wide enough to insert one end of the celery stick and stand it (on end), upward at an angle. It should resemble a tree trunk. Spread the remaining peanut butter on the apple slices and around the base of the celery tree to hold it in place.

Gently press an animal cracker (feet downward) into the peanut butter beneath the tree, so it appears to be standing by the tree (or climbing up it, depending on the animal).

Just watch as your kids gobble these up!

Store What You Eat, and Eat What You Store

Another great advantage to meal planning is that your family knows well ahead of time what they can expect for dinner. That means fewer pizza delivery calls or trips to the fast-food restaurants for a "quick bite to eat." That quick bite is usually a poor excuse for not planning ahead. I mentioned before that as I plan my menus, I go straight to my food storage shelves or my pantry and see what I have stocked. I make it a point to use at least one item from my pantry shelves for each meal, and sometimes two or three for a dinner idea. This way, I can be sure that my food is rotated regularly, and that we're really eating what we store.

Here's an example. I go into my pantry on Sunday afternoon, and I ask myself: What can I make this week with black beans or how can I incorporate bowtie pasta or lentils?

Generally the only foods I have to purchase during the week are the fresh fruits and vegetables that compliment my meals. Imagine how this concept can help lower your grocery bill. You're not buying on impulse; instead, you're implementing what you already have in your pantry. By purchasing a wide variety of nutritious foods, you can be sure that you'll be offering your family well-balanced meals. Never underestimate the power of a home-cooked meal! Believe me, it's much more than just the food that's served. It's the love that's put into it, and the conversation that's drawn out of your children as they sit around the dinner table admiring your latest creations!

Organizing Recipes

One of the biggest time-savers when implementing a menu-planning system is to organize your recipes. Whether you like to find recipes online, in magazines, or in recipe books, I suggest that you create a binder with all of your favorites. Each time you add a new menu item to your calendar, include it in your recipe binder. That way you'll never have to go digging through files, or try to remember exactly where you found that recipe that last time you made it. You may even like to categorize your binder like I do, filing the recipes under "Soups," "Beans," "Vegetarian," "Pasta," and "Salads," for example. This also saves a lot of time, because you don't have to write out each new recipe on a neat little recipe card that fits perfectly in your recipe box. You can simply copy, print, or tear out recipes from magazines or other sources and quickly slip them in a plastic sleeve. Done!

Leftovers and Casseroles

Two things I don't believe in: leftovers and casseroles. I usually make just enough food for a single meal, because I not only enjoy eating fresh, but I like my family to enjoy a variety of foods. I actually don't mind the dreaded question: "What's for dinner?" because all I have to say is "Look at the calendar!"

Now a quick word about casseroles. Try to eat foods that have more life and more fresh ingredients, and you'll naturally feel better. Foods that look attractive are more appealing than over-baked saucy mystery meals anyway. Isn't it refreshing to come to the table and see a fresh salad and food you're excited to put in your mouth, instead of vegetables out of a can and a steaming cheesy casserole? It's all in the planning, and you too can become a proficient menu planner if you just follow the steps I've shared with you.

Now about desserts—because everyone loves to finish off dinner with something sweet. I only plan three desserts a week. In fact, desserts are the only food that I don't mind serving as a leftover. They're great for kids' lunches, and the kids certainly don't complain about eating the same cookies for two or three days in a row! If you are one who doesn't mind leftovers, this may be a perfect way to supplement a lunch the next day, without having to prepare another meal.

A Note on Kids' Lunches

Do you ever find yourself caught between what your kids think is "cool" to eat for lunch and what you think is healthy for them to eat? Well, get them involved in the compromise.

Let's start with the sandwich. If it were up to our kids, they'd probably request PB&J on white bread. How about a healthier alternative? If you enjoy baking bread, whole grain is a better choice. However, if baking is not your forte, simply find a whole-grain bread that your kids will enjoy. Go lighter on the peanut butter, and even more lightly on the jelly, or just choose a healthier alternative altogether—perhaps turkey and cheese or chicken salad. Avoid foods like bologna, hotdogs, or processed cheese. They contain absolutely no nutritional value. Remember, what you feed the body, you feed the brain, so be selective!

The following list of substitutions could go a long way toward ensuring the choice of more nutritional foods.

Less Desirable Choice	Healthy Alternative
Sugary fruit snacks	Natural fruit leather
Candy	Dried fruit
Soda	Iced peppermint tea or lemon water
Popsicles	Frozen yogurt
Canned fruit	Precut fresh vegetables or fruits
Potato chips	Flavored popped wheat or whole-grain crackers with string cheese

Try to be consistent about adding fruits like grapes, apples, or orange slices along with baby carrots to lunches, because they're easy to prepare and give the kids a boost of vitamins.

Add a simple dessert or snack such as baked chips, granola bars, or dried fruit. Finally, top of the lunch with a healthy drink. If you offer your kids juice, be sure it's 100 percent natural, not a highly sugared juice blend. Milk is also a good option if they can purchase it at school, but try to avoid carbonated or caffeinated drinks altogether. Don't forget, there's nothing more natural than bottled water!

As I do my grocery shopping, I make sure that I'm always stocked with nutritious lunch ideas; that way, early school mornings run more smoothly. If your children are old enough to prepare their own lunches, organize their lunch supplies so that they're easily accessible and easy to prepare. Have a place for lunch sacks and plastic baggies, and a container for all the chips, snacks, drinks, and other fillers so that it's a one-stop lunch shop for your kids. Wash the fruit and vegetables ahead of time so that it's easy for them to pack as well. We all know that the more we can do at home to encourage our children to eat healthy, the better choices they'll learn to make once they're out on their own.

While all this planning may seem complex, it is truly simple, once you get the hang of it. My menu-planning only takes about fifteen minutes out of my Sunday afternoon. The rest of the time my family's napping, I enjoy baking a tasty dessert, or even some homemade bread. That way, I'm assured that when they wake up from their nap, there won't be any grumpies, and the tasty aroma gives my home a feeling of comfort and at-homeness. With my calendar ready, my weekly menu planned, and my grocery list tackled, I feel ready for a new week, organized and off to a good start. I pamper myself on Sundays by being the first one in bed—a fresh start to a new week!

Time to Take Action

1. Purchase a calendar with large-enough boxes on which to stick your menu tabs.
2. Write down your favorite menus on sticky tabs, and adhere them to your calendar.

3. Take inventory of your pantry and see which items you need to stock up on to be able to make your favorite meals several times. Include these items on your grocery list for the next few weeks.
4. Take a look at what your children are eating for lunch, and ask yourself if you could make any changes—healthier changes.

Get your family on the same page, and let them know what you are doing! Don't let husbands or kids break this system. You will have more time for them, and they will have a more sane wife and mother!

Chapter Two

Making the Most of Mondays

"Good ideas are not adopted automatically.
They must be driven into practice with courageous patience"
—Hyman Rickover

Seize the day! Now that you're organized and have your week planned, take a deep breath, and forge ahead. I like to start off my week with a clean house. If you're fortunate enough to have a maid, congratulations! For the rest of you, I'll share some helpful tips that will help you not only clean your home more efficiently, but also organize your home as you go. Remember, give yourself time to incorporate these ideas—they don't all have to be implemented at once.

I begin by listing those rooms that need to be cleaned. Whether it's dusting, mopping, vacuuming, making beds, doing laundry, or taking out the trash, I begin with a written list. This way, I can check things off as they're done, and it gives me a great sense of accomplishment. Turn on your favorite music (I love the opera for extra pep!), and get started.

Cleaning Checklist

Note: Not each item has to be done with each cleaning. Put a check mark in the first box to the left of column one if you plan to perform that task, and a check in the second box once you have completed it. Feel free to personalize your list to include other areas of your home as well as other tasks that might be required.

In the "delegate to" column, enter the names of the children to whom you would like to delegate the various jobs. Make them "age appropriate": that is, not beyond the child's ability. Check the first box to the left of column two when the assignment is given, and the second when the task has been completed.

		BEDROOMS			DELEGATE TO
		Take out trash	✓		
✓	✓	Clean bed linen			
		Collect laundry			
		Vacuum			
		Water plants			
		Dust furniture			
		BATHROOMS			
		Take out trash			
		Clean floors			
		Clean toilet			
		Clean sink(s)			
		Clean tub/shower			
		Clean mirrors			
		Dust vanity, etc.			
		Replace toilet paper			
		LAUNDRY			
		Iron clothes/linens/etc.			
		Spot clean			
		Sort socks			

Create a Cleaning Kit

If you have room, store an appropriate cleaning kit under each bathroom sink. The following is a list of the some items you may want to include.

2–3 clean rags	Liquid cleaner
Toilet brush and holder	Powdered cleaner
Small toothbush	Furniture polish

Window cleaner	Sponge or scrubber
Lemon disinfectant	Paper towels
Wastebasket liners	Air fresheners/refills
Extra toilet paper	Dust pan

I start in the bedrooms. While I encourage my children to clean their own rooms and make their own beds, some things I'd just rather do myself, such as vacuuming, watering plants, and sorting through "treasures" under the beds. As important as it is for kids to do chores, regardless of how many times standards are discussed, my twelve-year-old's version of clean and mine are two totally different things. So, I do end up in their rooms and bathrooms to make sure my standard of clean is met.

In each room, I pile everything that's disorderly onto their beds, and they can take care of the mess when they come home from school. As I move from room to room, I take three bags—one for trash, one for dirty laundry, and one for things that "simply belong somewhere else." Once that room is finished, I move on to the next, and by the time I'm done with each room, I have three bags full of things I know exactly what to do with. I haven't wasted any time running from room to room putting things in their right spot or running back and forth to the waste basket. Once all my dirty laundry is collected, I sort it out and begin the task of washing clothes. This works out great, because while the washing machine is going, I can move onto my next project, which is cleaning bathrooms.

Bathrooms

Don't you just love a clean bathroom? If equipped with the proper tools, you can enjoy a great smelling, germ-free bathroom in no time at all. Let me share some shortcuts I've learned. I have four bathrooms in my home, each on a different level, and the last thing I want to do is lug all of my cleaning supplies from bathroom to bathroom, so I've come up with a system that works great for me.

In each bathroom, I have a cleaning kit that I tuck under the cabinet. Each kit contains two or three clean rags, a toilet brush, a small toothbrush for hard-to-reach areas, a bottle of Windex, a lemon disinfectant, a pair of rubber gloves, several wastebasket liners, extra rolls of toilet paper, a roll of paper towels, and a package of plug-in aroma refills. While it sounds like a lot, it's the perfect solution to a spotless and clean-smelling bathroom in minutes! Once I launder the dirty rags, back they go under the sinks for the next cleaning. As I'll explain later, part of Saturday's cleaning is to be sure that all of these supplies are well-stocked! Having a cleaning kit for each bathroom also assures that no germs get transferred from bathroom to bathroom—smart, wouldn't you agree?

Laundry

Once the bathrooms are tackled, recheck your laundry, and put in another batch. Let me share with you how I keep my laundry organized and avoid huge piles of wrinkled clothes! Since I am home the whole time my laundry is being cleaned, it's easy for me to pull clean batches out of the dryer before they have a chance to get wrinkled. I immediately take them out and fold the clothes, placing each item in a labeled laundry basket up on a shelf. Each of my children has his own basket with his name. Their job is to retrieve their baskets, place the clean clothes in their rooms, and then replace the basket on the laundry room shelf. If any clothes need to be ironed, I simply make an "Ironing" pile and assign the pile to one of my children as an after-school job.

The Sock Challenge

I'm sure many of you have the challenge that I do of keeping track of stray socks. Well, here's an easy solution—I simply take another basket, labeled "lonely sock," and place all the clean socks inside. The task of matching up socks is a great way to keep a five-year-old entertained while he's waiting for dinner, by the way! This basket sits on the shelf right next to the kids' laundry baskets, so they're easy to find, and with four boys, I've learned that "easy-to-find" needs to be right under their noses!

After all the bedrooms and bedrooms are cleaned, I move on to the main living areas, leaving the kitchen for last. I grab two bags—one for trash and one for "things that belong somewhere else." This makes cleanup quick. I then vacuum the house, mop the floors, and end up in the kitchen. I clear off the counter and proceed to dump my "somewhere-else" bags out. Then I simply make piles for places where these things belong. For example "garage," "master bedroom," "laundry room," and so forth. In minutes, I can have all these stray items put away where they belong. Phew!

"Lost and Always Found"

Now, since I don't like every day to be a major cleaning day, I have a trick that I use that is very helpful. If you live on one level, choose a central place, perhaps a mudroom or linen closet, where you can easily access a small crate-size container to throw in "things that don't belong" on that level. If you have several levels in your home, perhaps you should consider one of these containers for every floor. I like to have a container with wheels. That way, I can easily cart it around the floor, and by the end of the day, I have collected all the things that don't belong, and ask each child to take a turn putting the items away. These things may include shoes, books, toys, papers, and trash. That way the home feels clean before everyone retires to bed, and I'm not left with a messy house in the morning. Another astonishing benefit to this system is whenever I hear my boys say (and I'm including my husband in that category), "Do you know where my [blank] is?" I automatically suggest that they check the lost-and-found container. Nine times out of ten . . . voila! There it is!

Built-In Maid Service

Now, lest you think I do all the cleaning myself, it's simply not true. I do have a maid service, and it's called "My Four Sons." Each of my boys is assigned three jobs after school. These jobs rotate throughout the week, and give each child an opportunity to master different skills. They include vacuuming, ironing, window washing, dusting, collecting trash, doing the laundry, washing floors, and emptying the dishwasher. I must say, never underestimate the power of a five-year-old. They too love to help with simple things like organizing clean silverware, matching socks, or taking out the trash. Starting them young gives them a sense of responsibility, not to mention pride in a job well done. Young children enjoy learning organizing skills, and love anything that has to do with spraying something out of a bottle. Let's capitalize on their enthusiasm. So, as they grow older, chores just become second nature. Demands of "Mom, can you . . . ?" diminish with more independent children. This prepares them in endless ways for when the time comes for them to venture out on their own as well. I will be confident in the knowledge that they can cook, organize, do their own laundry, and clean a toilet bowl all by themselves when they leave the comforts of home.

Tackling the Garage

I'm going to take organizing one step further. Do you often find that too many things get put in the garage and forgotten about because there's just nowhere else to put them? For example, library books and movies to return; items to exchange at the store, to donate to charity, or that are broken and need to be repaired; things you've borrowed from friends that need to be returned; dry-cleaning; and the list goes on. Instead of just letting these items stack up on my kitchen counter or clutter up my mudroom or garage, I make a special place for them close to where I park my car, so that as I come and go, I can regularly check which items need to be returned, donated, dropped off, or exchanged.

I like to use clear plastic drawers that stack. Each is labeled so that other family members know what's inside, and because it's a covered drawer, I can ensure that my items won't be damaged or soiled. You can place these stackable containers on a shelf or in a cupboard, and they're very space-friendly. The ones I use are approximately 18 inches wide, 20 inches deep, and 10 inches high. I can't tell you how much time this will save you, and the peace of mind that will come with knowing that each "stray" item will be accounted for. It takes just minutes to put together, and you'll love the convenience. In fact, these drawers are great to take right into the car with you—they're light, and they keep your items from falling off the seats. Give this a try and see how much clutter you can eliminate.

Refreshing the Refrigerator

Last and best of all comes the kitchen. Don't you love a clean kitchen? It seems that if my bathrooms are clean and my kitchen is clean, everything else just feels better, too.

At the top of my list is the refrigerator. If you find that you have leftovers when you go to clean out your refrigerator, why not eat those for dinner tonight, and save yourself another mess in your kitchen? I begin by taking everything out, and cleaning each shelf with a good disinfectant. I often find foods that I've forgotten about and that are just not fresh anymore. Discard any food that is past its prime and organize your refrigerator in a way that makes the most sense to you.

I like to organize my shelves in categories. Of course, produce, meats, and cheeses each have their own drawers. I devote one shelf strictly to foods that need to be eaten sooner rather than later, such as fresh berries, leftovers, or specialty items. Another shelf is dedicated to dairy products, such as yogurts, sour cream, cottage cheese, and so forth. All my condiments go in the doors, and another shelf is reserved for breads—bagels, buns, bread, rolls, tortillas, and the like. This way, my family knows exactly where things are, and if they cooperate, we have a nicely organized fridge, and things don't get piled up or squished to the back!

In chapter 3, I'll show you how simple it is to prepare all of your fresh produce once you get home from the grocery store. This frees up time for you during the week to make delicious and nutritious meals for your family, without spending all sorts of time cleaning, cutting, and preparing your vegetables at the last minute. It also helps your children to make better snacking choices, because foods are trimmed, cleaned, and ready to eat with very little effort. In order for your family to want to eat more fruits and vegetables, it's just got to be easier to pop in their mouths than unwrapping a candy bar or opening a bag of chips!

As I mentioned before, I like to have a cleaning kit under each cabinet in my bathrooms, and I do the same in my kitchen. I have my favorite cleaners, and I'm not afraid to use them! Once I've cleaned the kitchen from top to bottom, I take out all the trash that I've accumulated and sit down for a minute to relax. I look over my list of "things to do" and find great satisfaction in crossing off all the things that I've accomplished. The house feels clean, the laundry's done, my fridge is ready for brand-new groceries, and there's still lots of daylight left. Tomorrow will be just as productive, and you'll fall in love with your routine. Just make it your own, and enjoy the journey!

Time to Take Action

1. Make a master list of all of your home's cleaning needs. That way when cleaning day comes around, you simply circle the projects you want to focus on.
2. Create a plan that keeps you flowing from one room to the next without distractions when cleaning. Remember the "three bags" idea.
3. Make time to clean out your fridge once a week to optimize on space and keep it tidy and fresh.
4. Create your own cleaning kits for each bathroom and for your kitchen.
5. Put together a system close to where you park your car, where you can drop and pick up items that need to be returned.
6. Plan simple and healthy sack lunch ideas and perhaps organize a space that is designated for sack lunch items, so they're quickly accessible, even for your youngsters.

Chapter Three

Comfy-Shoes Tuesday

"You don't have to cook fancy foods or complicated masterpieces,
just simple foods from fresh ingredients"
—Julia Childs

Now that your refrigerator is spic-and-span, and you've prepared your grocery list ahead of time, you're ready to conquer the grocery store for fresh and delicious food. But this too needs to be done in an organized manner. Remember, go shopping on a satisfied stomach, so you won't be tempted to make purchases based on your cravings. Be sure to go armed with your list in hand, and try not to stray from that list. Best of all, be sure to wear comfy shoes, because you'll be doing a lot of walking!

Start with a List

A successful shopping trip begins with careful planning. I usually shop at one warehouse-type store, where I can purchase items in bulk, and then I choose a great grocery store, where I can purchase my fresh produce and deli items. Instead of coming up with a new grocery list every week, and trying to remember all the things I ran out of, I like to save myself time by making a master list for each of the two stores where I shop. Then I make several copies. I include everything that I would purchase at those stores and then categorize them. For example, "Dairy Products," "Frozen Foods," "Produce," "Cleaning Supplies," and so forth. Then I simply circle the items I need for that week, and I'm finished. I leave my list out during the week where it's handy so that whenever I run out of an item or think of something else I need to pick up at the store, I'll know exactly what those items are when I make my next shopping trip. This helps eliminate unnecessary stops throughout the week. When I create my master list, I make sure to list my items in order of aisles, so that once I'm at the store I can quickly go in order, find what I need, and not become distracted with the things I don't.

A sample shopping list (customize to your own needs):

Paper Products
Toilet paper
Paper towels
Garbage bags
Aluminum foil
Plastic wrap

Cleaning Supplies
Dish detergent
Laundry detergent
Fabric softener
General cleaners
Brushes/rags

Canned Foods
Fruits/vegetables
Soups
Meats
Sauces

Dairy/Eggs
Milk
Eggs
Sour cream
Cheese
Cream cheese
Yogurt

Produce
Apples
Bananas
Tomatoes
Lettuce
Potatoes
Herbs

Baking Supplies
Flour
Sugar
Chocolate chips
Salt/Spices
Oil

(List continues on next page)

Toiletries	Frozen Foods	Meats
Bar soap	Ice cream	Mixed lunch meats
Toothpaste	Juices	Ground beef/turkey
Deodorant	Vegetables/fruits	Chicken breasts
Lotions	Desserts	Roasts
Shampoo		Fish
	Boxed Goods	Sausage
Baked Goods	Cereal	Bacon
Bread	Crackers	
Rolls	Chips	
Bagels	Pasta	
Cookie dough		

Having an organized shopping list cuts my shopping time down significantly, leaves me extra time to fill up my car with gas, and get a car wash while I'm out.

Then I have the peace of mind knowing that not only is my fridge going to be well-stocked, but my car will also be as well. As soon as I get home from my shopping trip, I throw away the list I just used and pull out a new one. And the cycle starts all over again.

A Little Effort Goes a Long Way

Now let's discuss some "shopping day" habits. I mentioned before that cleaning your fridge before going grocery shopping is a great idea. This way you'll know exactly what you need, and you'll have plenty of space for fresh food. When you return from the grocery store, carefully put away each item so that it's convenient to use when you need it. For example, I take all of my produce out from the wimpy plastic bags they give me at the store, and I trim my vegetables, discarding any extra leaves, roots, or unwanted fluff. I don't wash my vegetables, but just give them a good picking-over, and then place them in better-quality containers or plastic bags. I like to vacuum seal the foods I'm going to freeze to maximize on their nutritional value. This helps them last longer as well.

21

Try cutting up your fresh vegetables, such as broccoli and cauliflower, into smaller snack-size pieces. I trim the ends and tops of my celery, and even peel a handful of carrots ahead of time and cut off the tops. That way they're easier to use when I'm in a hurry. If you purchase large quantities of meat, you may consider dividing them into meal-size portions, and individually wrapping them so that you don't have to fuss later with defrosting the whole package and then refreezing what you don't use. It's nice to know that all of your food is trimmed, preportioned, and ready to use, whether you're in a hurry or not. Another idea is to precook your meat, and then place it in individual meal-size portions in your freezer. This way, when you're pinched for time, all you have to do is quickly defrost your little package of precooked meat, instead of waiting for it to defrost and then preparing it to cook. A little bit of prep work in the beginning can save you a lot of work in the end.

Power Buying

Another habit I encourage is bulk purchasing. By this, I don't necessarily mean to buy all of you food in large quantities all the time. Instead, make it a habit to always buy one or two extra of the things that you use most commonly. For example, if you find yourself picking up a jar of peanut butter once or twice a month, consider just purchasing three or four at a time. Make an effort to pick out four or five items from your grocery list each week and do what I call "power buying," which is simply purchasing one or two extra of each of those items in one stop. Before you know it, your pantry will be bursting at the seams, and just that little extra effort will have paid off. If for some reason you can't make it to the grocery store one week, or your neighbor runs out of peanut butter, you'll be glad to know that you have that kind of insurance policy that allows you a little flexibility.

Taking Inventory

Having a pantry is "must" for any woman I know. However, as I have visited clients, friends, and family, almost all the pantries I've seen lack one important element—organization! They have become places for leftover chip bags, crumbling cookies, brooms, and cans of unused food that have been there for months! A pantry is the heart of a successful and organized kitchen. The food in the pantry should flow like the lifeblood of the heart, not remain stagnant. It's a constant practice of "shop, eat, replenish, repeat," as I call it! Remember, food storage is not food "hoardage."

One of the things that I find the most helpful in organizing a successful pantry is to have an inventory notebook. I like to know what I have and what I need. This ensures that my food is always fresh and that I'm rotating through my food in a timely manner. It also encourages me to attend case-lot sales and to watch for seasonal items that may be a good bargain. By writing down what I have and what I need, I never overbuy, and when I find that there is a great bargain on a certain item, like canned beans or canned tomatoes, I simply look at my inventory list, know exactly what I'm lacking, and how to supplement my supply.

This Is How You Do It:

Step 1: Begin with a blank sheet of paper. You can either do this all in one sitting, or you can place your paper on your fridge for a month, and write everything down that you consume in that period of time. Be specific, not leaving anything out. This will give you a pretty good idea of what you use regularly. If you're doing this exercise in one sitting, write down every item that you currently have in your pantry or food storage. The order is not important at this time. The organization comes later. Write down how much you have of each item. For example: "tuna—12 cans, rice—50 lbs, cake mixes—4 boxes."

Step 2: Write down everything you wish you had in your pantry or food storage. This can include candy bars, apple cider vinegar, canned salmon, or any other random item. Even those once-in-a-while foods you use for special recipes should be included in this list. This may really take some time, but don't leave anything out, because this all becomes your master list. You may want to browse through some of your favorite recipes to remind you of the foods you use, but usually don't stock.

Step 3: Determine how much of each of these items you or your family consumes in a one-month period, and multiply that by 3 if your goal is to have a three-month supply; by 6 if your goal is a six-month supply; or by 12 if your goal is a year's supply. Here's a simple example. We use two bottles of ketchup each month. I know that for a year's supply, I need to purchase twenty-four bottles of ketchup. Let's say I'm all out at the moment. Next time ketchup goes on sale, I'll buy twenty-four bottles at $0.99, instead of buying it one bottle at a time for $1.49. I've just saved myself $9.60 by purchasing my ketchup in bulk. While this may seem quite insignificant, you'll see that over time, this habit can save you hundreds of dollars, not to mention unnecessary time running back and forth to the grocery store.

Step 4: Categorize your list into food groups. For example, "Canned Fruits and Vegetables," "Canned Soups," "Condiments," "Baking Items," "Bulk Grains," and so forth. Next to each item in one column, write with a pen how much of that item you'll need to store for a year's supply. In the next column, with a pencil, write down how many units of that item you are lacking. Keep all of this data in a pocket-size notebook, and carry it with you in your purse when you shop. That way, when you see items on sale that you may need, all you have to do is whip out your inventory notebook, see if that item is on your list, and once you've purchased that item, erase and adjust your figures accordingly. Pretty simple!

Don't feel that you have to limit your inventory notebook to food. You may also find it helpful to dedicate a section to common household items such as toilet paper, paper towels, shampoo, batteries, deodorant, first aid supplies, and the list goes on! I've included a sample of what my inventory list looks like so you can get an idea of how this process works.

A sample inventory list:

Product	Current Inventory
Milk	Only 3 gallons, fresh
Cheese	Only 1 pound, fresh
Soy sauce	1 bottle
Ground beef	Only 2 pounds, fresh
Cereal	4 boxes
Spaghetti	10 pounds
Canned peaches	12 cans
Rice	25 pounds

As you compare your list of foods throughout your pantry, basement, and wherever else you may store them, you'll begin to ask yourself what you would do if you had to substitute those fresh foods like milk and cheese for the dried variety. You'll also ask how many of each item you would need to have in your storage to sustain you for one month, six months, or a year. As you compile this information, it will help you create an inventory notebook.

Below is a sample of what such a notebook might look like:

FOODS/ PRODUCTS	DESIRED SUPPLY	STILL NEEDED
Canned Fruits		
Peaches	36 cans	14 cans
Pears	36 cans	8 cans
Mandarin oranges	24 cans	18 cans
Canned Vegetables		
Corn	48 cans	12 cans
Black beans	36 cans	0 cans
Grains		
Wheat	1800 lbs.	1200 lbs.
Pasta	200 lbs.	100 lbs.
Rice	200 lbs.	0 lbs.
Popcorn	40 lbs.	0 lbs.
Condiments		
Soy sauce	4 bottles	1 bottle
Salad dressing	8 bottles	0 bottles

Getting to Know Your Pantry

When stocking your pantry, consider each item that you store, and challenge yourself to find out a way to use that item at least three different ways. This ensures that the item is being used regularly. For example, if you store raisins, find three different recipes where you enjoy using those raisins, so that they don't just sit on your shelf and dry out. It could be that you use raisins in cinnamon rolls, in granola, or just as an after-school snack for your kids. If you store garbanzo beans, find three recipes that you love where you could use these beans. Try to make a conscious effort to familiarize yourself with every food in your pantry, especially those that are extra healthy, but sometimes more challenging, like lentils, various grains, or dehydrated vegetables.

Become so familiar and comfortable with your food storage that it becomes an everyday way of life, rather than something to be dreaded in an emergency. I assure you that if you wait to eat your wheat or your powdered milk until the big earthquake hits or the world comes to an end, that will be your biggest emergency—your body will not know how to tolerate such foods, and you will learn very quickly what uncomfortable really means!

One more tip that will help make your pantry a success is making sure that your items are not running low. Although this is an activity that I leave for Saturday, I'll explain what I do in my home. I keep the bulk of my food supply downstairs in my basement where it's nice and cool. But next to my kitchen I have another room that's just a big walk-in pantry. Here I store smaller portions of the foods that I bring up from downstairs. Here they are easily accessible, and because I organize them in smaller containers, they are easy to transport from pantry to kitchen, or from pantry to basement, whenever I need to refill them.

For example, I store all of my larger buckets of grains, flour, sugar, and rice in cold storage. This way the shelf life is longer, and they stay cool and dry. I only bring up one bucket of each of these foods, and store them along the floor under all of my shelves in my pantry. Each bucket has it's own gamma lid—a plastic lid that includes a ring that snaps onto the top of the bucket, and also a screw top, that makes opening and closing these buckets simple and painless. Gamma lids provide an airtight seal, allowing food to stay fresh and rodent-free. I assign a different color gamma lid to each of my buckets. For example, yellow for flour, blue for sugar, red for wheat, white for rice, and so forth. When I run out of these supplies, I simply run down to the basement, bring up another full bucket, and dump it into the bucket that has the gamma lid. I do the same thing with my pasta and beans, only using much smaller containers.

If your family enjoys using a wide variety of pastas or beans, look for containers that are transparent and of the pull-out-drawer variety. They stack for more efficient spacing. It's helpful to label each one, and since they're small, they're easy to transport to the kitchen, or down to your basement for a refill. Store enough pasta and beans in these containers to last you a good four months.

Look at your shelving and consider what types of storage containers you could use to maximize your space. If you have not already built shelves in your pantry space, or the ones you already have are too far apart, you may consider adding more shelves or deciding what you'll put where so that you can fit as much food in your space as possible. Think about canned goods, dehydrated goods, cereals, buckets, juices, anything that you use. Try to create a system where everything is accessible and organized. I can't stress enough the power of a labeling machine. For around thirty dollars, this can fast become your best friend in your home as you begin to organize your belongings into containers, files, and boxes. Remember, the more organized you are, the more time you'll have to do the things you love, instead of being frustrated because of the chaos!

Time to Take Action

1. Create your own master grocery lists. If you go to several different stores, tailor one for each store, categorizing your items and listing them by aisle. Then copy enough so you can grab a new list every week.

2. Think of ways that you can prepare fresh fruits, vegetables, and meats into meal-size portions once you return from the grocery store, so you can save yourself time later.

3. Start an inventory list, regularly adding to it until you feel that you know exactly what you have on hand, and what you would like to start accumulating. Prepare an inventory notebook that you can tuck in your purse and start paying attention to sales.

4. Determine where you'll store the bulk of your food. The ideal is somewhere dry below 70°F (21°C). Then decide how you can take smaller portions of those foods, such as beans, grains, and pasta, and store them somewhere more easily accessible, like your pantry or kitchen.

5. Add more shelves, if you can, to maximize storage space.

6. Label containers so that you and your family know exactly what everything is.

7. Consider purchasing gamma lids to help preserve your bulk foods once they've been opened.

Watch out, you may fall in love with your labeler! I went through a time when I was so excited about organizing each cupboard and shelf in my kitchen, that I pulled a joke on my husband, labeling every spoon, every glass, every thing I could find, just to drive him crazy! When he came home, he exclaimed, "Anitra, what's going on here? Are we learning English as a second language?"

Chapter Four

Wise-Tips Wednesday

"Ideas are like rabbits. You get a couple and learn how to handle them, and before you know it, you have a dozen."
—William James

Who said comfy shoes were only reserved for Tuesday? You may need them just as much today! Wednesday is the day I schedule all of my errands. These include trips to the dry cleaners, post office visits, volunteering at my children's school, doctor's appointments, salon appointments, and so forth. By planning ahead, I quickly know what errands need to made. Remember those labeled containers in the garage we discussed in chapter 2? Those are also part of today. Because I've organized these containers in the garage, I can now easily grab those containers and know exactly what needs to be dropped off where. These errands are usually quick, and everything gets taken to its proper place—rented movies, dry cleaning, mail, and so on.

This day is also designated for bill paying and paperwork filing.

You may also wish to add phone calling to this list as well. It is a day to set up appointments, discuss questions about billing, or just make sure that all your affairs are in order.

I'm excited to share with you a filing system that has helped me tremendously. Do you have a pile in your kitchen that just seems to grow on its own, accumulating more and more paperwork—things you can't throw away, but you really don't know what to do with? Do you go through your children's backpacks after school, and wonder what to do with those reminder notes or school calendars? How about the mail that comes through your mailbox every day? Do you wish you had time to browse through your catalogs, and do you find yourself losing bills because they get lost in the shuffle? If you answered yes to any of these questions, then listen up—I think I may just have a solution for you that will not only save you time, but keep you organized and on top of all your paperwork.

Conquering the Paperwork

It all begins with a file box and some hanging folders. I suggest that you place this file in a place that is easily accessible—either in your kitchen, your pantry, or office—somewhere you pass every day, where you can easily drop in all your paperwork, mail, and the like. I will suggest how to label the tabs first, and then explain each one as we go. This exercise of filing paperwork will immediately eliminate the term "junk mail" or "junk pile." Make it a habit to pick up your mail from the mailbox only if you can give yourself two minutes to file it away appropriately. If not, wait till you have more time. As soon as you grab your mail, open each article, and decide where it will go.

Here Are My Suggestions

To Be Filed: This folder should come first. If you can do nothing else but sift through your mail and determine what needs to be kept for further looking, place it in this folder, and when you have extra time during the day, you can file it away where it belongs. At least it's off your countertop and in a safe place. Immediately throw the "junk mail" in the trash. If it's not important enough to be filed, don't give it a second chance!

Calendar: This folder is important. If you receive any party invitations, graduation announcements, anything that involves a calendar event, quickly write the event on your calendar, and then slip the invitation in this folder for later reference. You'll want to know the address of the party, and what to bring. If you have a bulletin board that you check regularly, this may also be a great place to pin up that invitation.

Financial: This folder will have three sub-folders. The first is labeled "To Be Paid." Here you file all your bills that come in. I encourage you to open each bill before you file it. Glance at it quickly to avoid shock later, then throw away the original envelope, and neatly tuck the bill inside the return envelope. You can go as far as to prestamp your envelopes as you file them away, so that when they're ready to go, they're ready to go. I like to note on my wall calendar when each bill is due, so that I can quickly go to my file and pull out that bill and be sure it goes out on time. The second folder will be labeled "Coupons." If you have time to quickly go through a classified add and clip a coupon that interests you, this is where it goes. Also, gift certificates to restaurants or movies, for example, can be filed here. The last folder is labeled "Receipts." You will find this folder to be invaluable, especially when making large purchases. You'll know that your receipts are always in one place, should you ever have to make a return, and you won't panic later down the road. I even like to take this one step further and make separate envelopes for each month. Once they're labeled, I can easily go back and find which month I made a certain purchase, and quickly find the receipt. Another possibility is to label envelopes according to store. You certainly have your favorites, and you'll find that sometimes it's easier to find a receipt if you just remember where it was purchased. Regardless of the system you use, you'll have peace of mind.

Bills Paid: Once you've paid your bills, you'll want to be sure to write down on your receipt portion of the bill the date that it was paid, and then tuck it away in this folder. I like to file my bills by month, and so I simply keep them together with a large paperclip. If there's ever a question on a previous bill, I can find it in seconds, instead of having to shuffle through endless piles of paperwork. Once the year is over, I gather all twelve piles of these "bills paid," and I slip them into a manila folder with the year written on the outside. This then goes into a box for safe-keeping.

Taxes: This is an important file folder to have, because you can drop all your receipts for purchases that are tax-deductible throughout the year. Keep your mortgage statements, company deductions, and charitable donations so that at the end of the year, you can simply hand this whole file over to your accountant, and let him take care of it.

Family: Take one folder for each member of your family, and label their names on each one. This way you can file away any important papers that are particular to that person. These papers may include special artwork from school, personal cards or certificates of achievement, photographs, or anything else that I'd like to safeguard. This is especially helpful when the children come home from school with important papers, and you just don't want them to sit on your countertop. Your children will know that if they are missing something, or they want anything to be safe, this is their own personal space.

Among all of my boys, we collect a lot of scout merit badges, and what better place to keep them all together than their own file folder? When I get time to actually sew them on to their uniforms, I know exactly where to find them and they're clean and organized. These files are also handy for special art projects, school certificates, and photos I want to transfer to their treasure boxes later on.

It may surprise you that all of these folders can easily fit into one average file box. It takes up very little space, but it can really take the headache out of everyday paperwork. Everything has its place, and you live uncluttered!

Once you've created this basic filing system, you may want to expand it to include more folders. I have a different file box that is fire-proof, where I keep my most important papers. These are some examples: mortgage statements; bank statements; identification papers such as birth certificates, social security cards and passports; health and life insurance contracts; investment information; contractors I use for home improvement projects; keepsakes; warranties; and the list goes on.

I challenge you to take control of your paperwork by trying this simple filing system. I promise that once you get started organizing and de-cluttering, you'll find that taking care of the busywork just got a whole lot easier. You'll love knowing right off the top of your head where all those important documents are. You won't spend countless hours when tax season comes along searching for all your important papers.

Creating a Mini Office in Your Kitchen

All of us have a "junk drawer" in the kitchen—a place where we dump all our writing tools, scissors, junk, junk, and more junk. Well, let's clean it up and make a really useful space! Why not turn this drawer into the most efficient office space you can? This way you'll have everything you'll need for card-writing, calculating, mailing, and filing right at your fingertips. In fact, because this little drawer usually has a cabinet underneath, you may be able to use that cabinet space for the file box you've just created!

Begin by purchasing four containers with shallow sides. The ones I use are approximately 5 inches wide, 8 inches long, and 2 inches deep. I like to use plastic, because my labels adhere easily and I can clean them out with soapy water when they get messy.

The first container is labeled "Pens/Pencils." It's obvious what I fill this with. Make sure to keep markers, colored pencils, or any other artsy writing utensils in another place. We'll discuss an "Activity Center" in chapter 6 where these can be stored. Start fresh by purchasing your favorite pens and pencils. I don't particularly like pens with lids, because somehow the lids always end up on the floor, or somewhere else in the drawer. So be selective. If you purchase pencils, you may consider the kind with the refillable lead, so that you don't have to mess with sharpening pencils so often.

The second container is labeled "Tools." I find it invaluable to have simple tools in my kitchen. These include a couple of screwdrivers, a small box of nails, razor blades, batteries, a measuring tape, and any other simple tools you find yourself using regularly. Just remember, your box is only so big. There's no room for that cordless screwdriver you got for Christmas!

The third box is labeled "Office." This includes items such as scotch and masking tape, a calculator, a roll of stamps, address labels, sticky notes, a box of paper clips, a ruler, a stapler, scissors, and any other items you may need to make your office space more convenient.

The last box is labeled "Misc." Notice I didn't use the word "Junk"! As you clear your countertops during the day and find small items that don't belong, drop them in this container, and when it's full, find a home for them. These items will probably include your husband's watch or cell phone, some spare change, your kid's extra house key, and so forth. The rest of the drawer gets divided into sections for mailing envelopes, stationary, and larger items like a labeler and your address book.

By teaching your family how this drawer functions, (and I don't mean opens and closes), you will all benefit by having the tools you need when you need them.

A Key in Time Saves Your Mind

Just a quick word about that cabinet below your "office drawer." Why not make that your "spare key" department? Simply use the door to the cabinet as a place to hang several hooks. I like to use the hooks with the sticky tape on the back because they are easily removed if need be. Over each hook, I stick a label, such as "house," "cars," "motorcycle," "storage unit," "sports rack," and so forth. Then I make several copies of each key, and hang them on their appropriate hooks. This is the perfect place to look when you're husband's late for work and can't find his keys, or when your teenager has accidentally dropped the keys inside the sports rack. Just a thought!

Reach Out and Touch Someone

Start today—if you feel you're not perfect at anything, you can be perfect at this! Now I've talked a lot about organization and paperwork in this chapter, but one kind of paperwork I feel very strongly about is personal mail. I love to write it, and I love to receive it. Doesn't it make you feel great when you sift through all your junk mail to find a handwritten note addressed to you personally? That absolutely brightens my day, and so I have tried to make it a habit to write a simple card once a week to a friend or a neighbor. It also helps me to be more conscious of kindnesses that happen all around me, and I'm grateful for that. Having a stash of attractive stationary close by for moments like these is helpful, and because this day is a day for the post office, you can make sure to pick up a book of stamps as well. If you find you'd rather make a personal phone call to express your love or your gratitude to someone, or send a quick e-mail, that's another great way to recharge your battery as well as someone else's. But just think—by writing a card, you'll be making a great contribution to someone else's personal file!

Time to Take Action

1. Make a list of errands you typically run during the week and try to schedule them all for one day. Also try to schedule appointments for a single day.
2. Catch up on phone calls for things like appointments and bills.
3. Purchase a file box and begin putting together your folders. Eliminate clutter by filing your paperwork as soon as it comes into your hands.
4. Create a mini-office drawer in your kitchen and teach your family how to use it. Consider making copies of keys as a backup for stressful times.
5. Put aside time each week to go through your file box, and update what needs to be done.

___ 6. Purchase some attractive stationary and colorful stamps so that you can share a few kind words every week. See what a fun habit this can become and how much this simple gesture can lift others.

Chapter Five

Celebrate Thursdays

"Take rest. A field that is rested gives a bountiful crop."
—Ovid

I absolutely love Thursdays and schedule all my favorite things for this day. Whether it's lunch with friends, shopping for a special gift, or taking a long bubble bath, this day is all mine, and I look forward to it all week!

Like any other day, if this day is not scheduled out, it seems to get away from me too fast. I think we all need a day to unwind, to recharge, and to relax for a change. Even if it's just two or three hours, a time to get in touch with yourself will not only help you relax, but you'll gather energy for the rest of the week. It's also a great way to reward yourself for all the hard work you put in the first four days of the week. Here are some suggestions:

- ♥ Take a long bubble bath
- ♥ Listen to beautiful music
- ♥ Take a nap
- ♥ Have lunch with a friend
- ♥ Go shopping for a special someone
- ♥ Write in a "Thankful journal"
- ♥ Skip your workout at the gym
- ♥ Sleep in
- ♥ Browse through your favorite recipe books
- ♥ Find a quiet place to curl up with a great book
- ♥ Indulge in a decadent dessert
- ♥ Do no housework
- ♥ Dress up for no reason
- ♥ Plan a vacation
- ♥ Get a massage

Laughter, I find, is a great way to unwind, and there's nothing I love more than spending time with a friend who is witty and entertaining. Even if it's just one hour over lunch, I love to spend time talking to an adult and laughing about the parodies of life. Other times, however, I love solitude and enjoy listening to my own thoughts. Being in nature helps me clear my head and appreciate the beauty that surrounds me. I pretend that no obligations are waiting for me at home, no phone calls to return, no deadlines to make. I focus on the moment and wish that time would just stand still.

If you are used to exercising every day, decide to take a break today, and relax in a yummy bubble bath instead. Take longer getting ready, and sing to yourself! If you sound great, this will lift your spirits. If you don't, sing anyway—it's great therapy! Now, remember all those catalogs and magazines you get in the mail that you file away in your handy-dandy file box from chapter 4? Well, this is a perfect day to pull them out and browse through them. Tear out new recipes to add to your menu calendar, plan a vacation, or get new decorating ideas for your home. Whatever you do, just enjoy the moment!

Reach Inward by Reaching Out!

Someone once said, "The fragrance always stays in the hand that gives the rose." I believe that sometimes the best thing I can do for myself is to do something for someone else. I look forward to Thursdays, because I plan to dedicate part of my day to helping someone else. We all have a gift. You may be a musician, an artist, a great cook, or even a wonderful reader. Why not share that gift with someone who really needs it? I have found that one of the most precious gifts you can share is the gift of listening. This is truly an art, and if practiced regularly can be a true blessing for people in your circle of influence.

One of my favorite activities is to visit the senior care center where my darling Aunt Coral lives. There are handfuls of elderly residents who sit in the lobby just waiting for someone to reach out and say hello. Some are sharp in their memory, while others simply moan and dribble, but still, they all long for a friend. I like to learn their names, and then offer to entertain them on the piano with the timeless music of Chopin, Debussy, Beethoven, and others. They all scoot their wheelchairs a little closer, and some even begin to hum the melodies that they remember. After each selection, they lift their feeble arms to clap, and ask for "just one more, please, just one more!" After an hour, it is hard to say good-bye, without wishing I could just pack them all in my car and take them home with me. They are gracious and kind and I consider them some of my dearest friends.

If you have extra time today, consider preparing a delicious yet simple meal for your family. Even fancy take-out by candlelight can be fabulous! Throw in a decadent dessert, and pamper your family tonight. But let them do the dishes for a change!

At last, slip into a pair of your favorite pajamas just a little earlier than usual, and if you can, sneak off to bed before everyone else does! I promise you, stepping out of your routine is good for you, and should be guilt-free! Give it a try, and see how refreshing your Thursdays can be!

Time to Take Action!

1. Plan your pampering day. Whether it's hours, or just a few moments, treat yourself to a little rest and relaxation. You'll be amazed how it will recharge you!
2. Consider involving someone else in your plans today. Share the gift of your time and reach out to those who need your smile.
3. Treat your family to a cozy candlelight dinner tonight, and love their reaction.
4. Invest in a great pair of comfy pajamas, and go to bed early tonight. Dream of what you'll treat yourself to next Thursday!

Chapter Six

Friday, and Almost Finished!

"The best way to keep children home is to make the home atmosphere pleasant—and let the air out of the tires."
—*Dorothy Parker*

Welcome to the weekend! You've had a busy week, and it's almost over. But just a few loose ends remain to tie up. Because I don't like to spend my whole Saturday cleaning house, I get an early start and involve my children by getting the inside of the house nice and clean before the weekend gets into full swing. I divide up the chores, and even bribe them to do a few extra tasks, promising to reward them with treats or movies while my husband and I go out for a date.

Activity Center

I have found that organizing an activity center for my young children has been a great lifesaver while we're gone. This way they're not stuck in front of the television for hours. And if there's a babysitter, they'll have something to do with the children that's creative and fun. It's quite simple to put together. If you have a linen closet or an entertainment center that has some extra space, that's a great place to start. You could also use one of your children's closets (just find a spot that won't be taken over by dirty clothes or buried by toys).

Begin by stocking a generous supply of construction paper of every color. Place the papers in a box so they don't get bent. You may want to purchase three or four plastic containers and label each with different items. Markers, crayons, and colored pencils in one; glue, tape, and scissors in another; and staplers, paper punches, stickers, and glitter in another. During the week, as you're throwing things away, such as empty toilet paper or paper towel rolls, plastic milk caps or other recyclable items, ask yourself if they could be used by your children for a creative art project. If so, place these items in a box as well. They're always surprised to find new things. Remember, before throwing out large boxes, see if you can flatten them down, slip them under a bed, and save them for a rainy day. These boxes can be made into the most magnificent forts and princess castles!

Challenge your children's creativity, and they can come up with all sorts of things to do. One of my children's favorite activities is playing with play dough. You can make the recipe with items you already have in your pantry. Here is the recipe:

Anitra's Play Dough Mix

Combine the following in an airtight container:
6 cups all-purpose flour
3 cups salt
2 Tbsp. cream of tartar

When ready to make the play dough, simply bring 1 cup water to a boil in a small saucepan. Add several drops of your child's favorite food coloring, along with 1 tablespoon oil and 1 cup of the play dough mix. Stir the mixture briskly over medium heat for about 60 seconds, until the dough forms into a soft ball. Once all ingredients are incorporated and smooth, carefully remove the dough ball from the pan onto your countertop, and allow to cool several minutes before handling, as it will be quite hot. Knead it several times to make sure it's nice and smooth, and then hand it over to the kids and let their imaginations run wild!

You can also try several different colors, and seal them in plastic bags. This recipe is great because it stays soft for months, and all you have to do is pack a handful of cookie cutters, a few rolling pins, and several plastic knives in an art box, and away they go. This is also a great activity for kids when they have friends over and start feeling bored or have nothing to do on a rainy day. They mold everything from their favorite cartoon characters to little monsters and funny animals.

Of course a great variety of puzzles, board games, and card games are always a welcome activity for kids, especially older ones. If you have a designated playroom with space for a card table, try putting out an age-appropriate puzzle on the table with the frame already put together. It will surprise you how often little ones will wander over to the puzzle table and try to fit pieces together, after getting bored of watching television or playing with other toys.

Speaking of television, I have found that home movies are a great change of pace. They're always a great way to entertain children—after all, who doesn't love to laugh at themselves on the screen? Be sure that you label each movie, however, and date them so that these priceless treasures don't end up in another CD case. Encourage your children to take out only one game at a time, one movie at a time, or one toy at a time, so that cleanup is quick, and parts don't get mixed up. Of course, if your family is like mine, this practice only works about half the time, but it's a good habit to instill in young children, nonetheless.

Last, but not least, I find that this activity closet should include some tasty treats. Do you ever feel frustrated because you're running late and your kids want movie treats or friends come over to play unexpectedly, and there are no fun snacks in the cupboard? Make a special place in this closet for such times, and you'll always have them on hand when you need them. Be sure to separate these treats from your regular pantry space, because the pantry seems to be free reign for whomever, whenever—especially dads! Pack items that aren't really messy—fruit leather, popcorn, dried fruit, boxes of raisins, bags of nuts, bottled water, and other snacks that aren't loaded with sugar. I make sure to let the family know that these snacks are off-limits except for playdates and movie nights.

Can you see how planning ahead can really pay off when you need peace of mind the most? You'll love to know that your children look forward to your leaving the house as much as you do on a Friday night, and that you are calm and relaxed, thanks to some forethought!

Ideas for children's activities using things you already have around the house:

Rain Sticks

1 empty cardboard paper towel roll
colorful yarn
Elmer's glue
⅓ cup of rice and small beans, mixed
6 flathead pins
scissors
1 piece of card stock
pencil
masking tape

Begin by tracing a circle with the pencil on the card stock around the end of the paper-towel tube.

Cut out two circles of card stock—one for each end of the tube. Place aside.

Following the curved seam along the length of the cardboard tube, insert flat-head pins into the tube about ¼-inch apart from the top of the tube to the bottom, in a spiral pattern. When the beans and rice "sift through" the rain stick, it creates that lovely rain noise!

When finished, cover the pins with a long strip of masking tape to prevent them from coming out.

Then tape one of the round pieces of card stock to one end of the tube.

Dump the mixed rice and bean mixture into the tube and then tape the second circle of card stock to the open end of the tube.

Starting at one end of the tube, begin gluing and wrapping the yarn in a circular pattern. Keep the yarn tight and close together.

When all is wrapped, allow to dry completely.

If you like, you can attach a braided piece of yarn to each end of the rain stick and make it into a carrying strap or a necklace!

Homemade Ice Cream

• •

½ cup milk
½ tsp. vanilla
6 Tbsp. rock salt
½ bag ice
1 Tbsp. sugar
1 quart-size plastic bag
1 gallon-size plastic bag

Pour ½ cup milk, ½ teaspoon vanilla, and 1 tablespoon sugar into a quart-size plastic bag.

Seal tightly and place bag into the larger gallon-size bag that is filled halfway with ice and 6 tablespoons rock salt. Seal tightly.

Shake the bag vigorously for 5 minutes (passing it from child to child to get them involved), until soft ice cream forms.

It's creamy, yummy, delicious!

Dinosaur Fossils

. . . .

    1 medium mixing bowl
    Several small plastic dinosaur toys
    1 spray bottle containing water
    2 cups plaster of paris
    ½ cup water
    4 cups play sand

Begin by combining 2 cups of plaster of paris with ½ cup water. Set aside.

Place the play sand into the bowl and mist it lightly with water to make a dripping consistency.

Place the dinosaur toy on its side into the moist sand, pressing gently.

Carefully remove the toy, and pour the plaster of paris mixture into the indentation left by the toy.

Allow the plaster to dry completely and remove the "fossil" from the sand.

Brush excess sand off gently, and you've got yourself a little home-made treasure!

Edible Ocean

. . . .

    Glass bowl (preferably a small fish bowl)
    Blueberry Jell-O (for "water")
    Water
    Candy Swedish fish or gummy sharks
    Shoestring licorice (for "seaweed")

Follow the recipe on the Jell-O box to make blueberry Jell-O.

Pour the mixture into a glass bowl or small fish bowl.

Gently lay the shoestring licorice at the bottom of the bowl to resemble seaweed.

When the Jell-O is almost set, place the Swedish fish or gummy sharks into the "water" so they appear to be swimming.

Just think—You'll never have to feed these little fishy friends.

This can also be made as a party favor inside a cellophane gift bag!

Time to Take Action!

1. Organize a children's activity center. Include crafts, games, books, puzzles, movies, and of course, tasty treats.

2. As you shop, consider purchasing items that might be on clearance and could be a great surprise in your activity center—items like inflatable balls, bottles of bubbles, and paint-by-numbers, just to name a few.

3. Explain to family members that keeping this space clean and organized is a joint effort, and be sure to stock up on new items regularly so you're not caught off guard.

Chapter Seven

Squeezing in Saturday

"By perseverance, the snail reached the ark."
—Charles Spurgeon

It seems we never have enough Saturdays in the month. This is the day we rush to get everything done so we can relax on Sunday! Saturday at my home is broken down into two parts—working and playing. This is a great day for yard work or home improvement projects. You surely have your list of "honey-do's" as well. While my children deep clean their rooms and mow the lawn, my husband and I generally take care of things around the house that need repairing or upgrading. We usually try to fill our morning with home projects, so that by lunchtime we can give it all up for a fun activity with the family. What are things that take priority for you on Saturdays?

Divide and Conquer

As I mentioned earlier, each member of the family has his own chores today, but I make sure to start them all off with our traditional breakfast—Classy Crepes and an Oh, So Orange Smoothy. Once their tummies are full and everyone's happy, we're off to a running start. I've included these scrumptious recipes below:

Classy Crepes
• •

In a blender, combine the following:

> 4 eggs
> 1½ cups water
> 1 cup milk
> 2 tsp. vanilla
> 2 cups flour
> ½ tsp. salt

In a dry hot skillet, pour a thin coat of batter, and wait till bubbly. Turn gently and brown on the other side. Serve with cinnamon sugar or cream cheese and sliced pears. Makes 24.

Oh, So Orange, Smoothy
• •

In a blender, combine the following:

> 1 16 oz. can orange juice concentrate
> 4 scoops vanilla ice cream
> 3 cups milk
> 1 Tbsp. vanilla
> A handful of ice cubes
> Enough water to almost fill the blender

Blend together until smooth, and serve immediately. Makes 6 servings.

If we have all done our work throughout the week, Saturday jobs should be quite simple. I start by sending each child to his room for a deep clean, which includes picking up trash, stripping the sheets, dusting, and vacuuming. Within about thirty minutes, they're done, and I move them on to a bigger project. My teenagers generally take care of the yard work, while the younger boys do inside jobs, like cleaning handprints off the walls, sorting socks, sweeping the garage, and helping me with my favorite job—stocking the shelves.

Stocked and Ready

The task of stocking shelves can be rewarding because it makes you feel like you just got back from the grocery store, without even leaving your house! Start with all the bathrooms, making sure that each one has an ample supply of toilet tissue, cleaning supplies, and that things like burned-out light bulbs and trash liners are replaced. Check to see that each bathroom has plenty of clean towels and a good supply of soap, shampoo, and bubble bath on hand for the coming week. You may consider storing all of these items in the same general area of your home so that restocking is quick and that you know exactly what you're running low on without having to check inside each cupboard.

Next, move on to the kitchen. Take a minute to check that all your cleaning bottles are full, and that you have clean rags for cleaning day on Monday. Change the vacuum bag if it's full, and replace the furnace filters if needed. Remember the series of boxes we organized in the garage earlier? Well, check the box labeled "things to be repaired," and take care of those. This includes buttons that need to be sewn onto shirts, books that are torn and need to be taped, and the list goes on and on.

Finally, end up in the pantry. As I mentioned before, I keep the bulk of my food storage downstairs in my basement where it's nice and cool. I also store smaller amounts of these foods upstairs in my pantry. Today is the day where I "go shopping" downstairs. In other words, I check my shelves in the pantry to see which items need to be replenished. Whether it's canned foods, cereals, grains, pastas, snack foods, or whatever, I simply go down in my basement and fill up what's missing. Again, my younger children like to participate. They each grab an empty grocery bag, and start filling and restocking. Remember, when you bring newer food into your pantry, be sure to stock your shelves from the back so that what comes in first goes out first. In other words, stack your cans only four or five deep, and no more than eight inches high, so that you can easily stock your items from the back. If you have slanted shelves, where the cans roll forward as you take them from the front, you've got it very easy!

Sugar and Spice, and Everything Nice!

Spices are a staple all their own, and should be treated with extra care. If you find yourself frustrated with your spice drawer because all of the containers are mismatched, or you just don't have an organized way to find them when you need them, let me share with you a system that is simple and clean!

Begin by pulling out all of your containers. Open them one by one and smell them. Are they still fragrant? Is the color good, or have they been in the drawer since Aunt Betty bought them ten years ago for Thanksgiving dinner? Once you've determined which spices to keep and which to toss, I suggest that you find a container that is perfect for your space. For example, I keep my spices in a small drawer close to my stove. I line it with a gripper pad so that my bottles stay in their place as I open and close the drawer. The best advice I can share with you on storing herbs is twofold.

First, purchase fresh spices. The spices that you find on the grocery store shelves are not usually fresh. They have been sitting in a warehouse for months, and may have a pretty label, but that is most often deceiving. I find that purchasing herbs in bulk from a reputable spice company is always the best thing. I recommend companies like San Francisco Herb Co. or Penzey's Spice Co. By purchasing in bulk, you'll only have to worry about ordering once a year, and you'll always have enough on hand to quickly refill your containers. If you have an extra refrigerator, I would suggest that you store the bulk of your spices there. Take out only as much as you'll use within a three- or four- month period and store it in smaller containers in your kitchen. This way you can ensure the freshness and the potency of your herbs and spices.

Second, only store your spices in glass jars. These can be purchased from the vendors I mentioned above. The reason for using glass is that plastic robs the integrity of the flavors by absorbing them into the plastic. Look at the height of your spice drawer, and choose the tallest jar that will fit in the drawer. My favorite size is 2 ½ inches tall by 2 ½ inches in diameter. Fill your containers, and then divide them into categories, leaving a little space between each grouping for wiggle room. I sort mine into groups like these: "Sweet Spices," "Savory Spices," "Salts and Peppers," "Herbs," and "Others." Once the lids are labeled, it's easy for me to find just the spice I'm looking for, without having to turn each container around, and fuss with shuffling through endless bottles.

Digging Deeper

Now that you're on a roll and excited about organizing your spice drawer, you may be hungry for some more easy tricks to spiffy up other kitchen cupboards and drawers!

Let's talk about your "Pots and Pans" cupboard. Do you find yourself digging and burrowing through this cupboard each time you need a saucepan? Have you considered purchasing a rack for your lids that simply screws on to the inside of your cupboard door? That way the lids are easily accessible, and you can stack your pots and pans inside each other. Problem solved! Move your larger or less-frequently used pots to the back and slide the more popular ones to the front.

What about your utensil drawer? I mean the one where you throw all your wooden spoons, wire whisks, potato mashers, and so on. Take a closer look at these items and ask yourself how many rubber spatulas or pancake flippers you really need. I have found, as an avid cook, that I never need more than two of the same utensils at the same time. My motto is "buy new, discard the old." As much as Aunt Betty's orange spatula means to you, it doesn't do you any good if it's melted at the end or if the handle is broken. Learn to let things go! When you purchase new cooking utensils, consider better-quality tools, and fewer of them. You'll be glad you did!

Another tip is not to store your cooking utensils in a crock on your countertop. As beautiful as that crock may be, it's just a magnet for dust, bugs, and grease to settle where they really don't belong. Instead, place these items in a drawer close to your stove top. This drawer should be fairly shallow and long in order to best fit all of your utensils. Starting at one side of the drawer, group all of your cooking utensils by kind. Spatulas; whisks; wooden spoons; ladles, and so forth. Reserve the back of the drawer for tools you use less frequently, such as potato mashers, pie cutters, and so forth.

Let's also consider your "plastic containers" drawer. This drawer, in my opinion, can be the most challenging. The problem is how to stack all those plastic storage containers while keeping track of lids ranging in color and size. Again I ask you, how many of these containers do we really need? May I suggest that you empty out this drawer or cupboard and start from the top. Try to find a matching lid for each container. If there is no match, place that container aside. Once you've determined which containers you'll keep, store them inside one another according to shape and size. Round containers together, square together, and so on. Now take one of the "extra" containers that didn't have a lid and fill it with all of the lids that go with the containers you do have. Each time you need a storage container, you'll know where to find just the right size and locating the matching lid will be a breeze. There you go!

Finally, one more tip for a more organized kitchen. Take care of your extras! Let me explain. How often do you open a bag of marshmallows, chocolate chips, peanuts, or another popular item, and then twist the bag and set it on the shelf? Quite often these items stack up or get shoved to the back of the cupboard just to be forgotten. Meanwhile, because you forget that they're back there, you cut into a new bag. Wouldn't it make more sense to store these items either in labeled plastic containers with twist-tops, where they can easily be taken out of their original packaging and stored, or even simpler, couldn't you just designate a specific basket or box for these items? That way, you'll know to check the basket of extras first before you open a brand-new package. Instead of twisting the half-opened bags and hoping the items won't fall out, take a minute to wrap an elastic around the top to preserve the freshness of your foods and to prevent dust or critters contaminating them.

Doesn't that feel great? Can you begin to see how much more you'll enjoy working in the kitchen, once your space is more organized? Remember, take small steps toward neatness. Tackle one drawer or cupboard at a time, and before you know it, your whole kitchen will be tidy and manageable.

Well, back to my Saturday! By noontime, I feel like I've accomplished a lot. My children's bedrooms are cleaned, all the sheets are freshly laundered, the lawn is mowed, the shelves stocked, and my husband has surely either fixed a home disaster, or created one! After a quick lunch, we're off to play! Whether it's playing at a friend's house or spending time with the family on an excursion, it's important for everyone to unwind and let loose.

At the end of this day, we love to watch a movie together, and just relax. It's nice to know that things are in order, and we all look forward to a relaxing Sunday!

Time to Take Action!

1. Begin today with a great breakfast. Create your own tradition.
2. Make a list of chores that need to be done. Divide and conquer.
   Be sure to put a time limit on work today, so you have time to enjoy some R&R.
3. Have fun! Play together, and get rid of tension. Unwind. Relax.

Congratulations!

You've come to the end of your week, and look at all that you've accomplished! Can you see your progress? Have you come up with ways to implement these organizing tips into your everyday life? I hope that you've enjoyed this little journey through "A week in the life of Anitra" and that you feel motivated to take action!

I promise you that as you begin to implement these ideas in your everyday life, you'll find time you didn't think you had and energy you didn't know could be yours. You will free up more time for things and people you love, and you will feel a peace of mind that comes with being prepared and organized.

Remember, only you can decide to put these principles into action.

You are the key to your success!

Live smart, Live simple, Live well!

Testimonials

Who knew organizing and planning your life could be so much fun? These secrets I have learned from Anitra won't stay secrets for long—I want to share what I've learned with everyone I know so that their lives can also be enhanced.

> —Rebecca McDonald

Anitra is a delightful, enthusiastic walking encyclopedia of food storage, nutrition, and helpful tips around the kitchen. Her classes not only hold your interest, but grab your attention, creating within you a desire to do something great about your family's health and well being.

> —Dan G.

Food Storage overwhelmed me until I heard Anitra's enthusiastic and passionate approach, which was refreshing compared to the other classes I'd experienced! She knows storage benefits first hand and uses her food storage on a daily basis. Anitra's expertise is well worth your time and money if you are serious about starting or improving your food storage system.

> —Jill Van Dyken

Anitra is a natural at teaching skills for food storage and organization. My husband and I took her classes and finally learned how to make yogurt the right way! She has a unique way of involving her audience with her fun personality and knowledge of food preparation and storage.

—Linda and George Thompson

Anitra inspired me to transform the mundane clutter of my life into a peaceful oasis of order. Thank you, Anitra. You seemed to be reading my mind!

—Monique Mead

Who ever would have thought that a cooking class on beans could be so fun? I never thought I could be so inspired about food storage. Anitra makes it look so simple, her food presentation is amazing, and the food tastes delicious! Don't miss out!! After going to three classes and coming home so excited, my husband was anxious to come and see what all the fun was about. It turned into a memorable date night!!!

—Melissa Sanchez

Anitra has helped me get my family organized. I love that Anitra inspired me to build up and use a food storage system through her wonderful classes. It makes me feel good that I now have not only the food, but the skills to take care of the ones I love!

—Katty Dowdle

I thought food storage was only for a rainy day disaster, but now I've learned how to use and rotate my food storage for all my days! Thanks Anitra for your inspiration—you are the DIVA!

—Sheri Robison

I now understand what is meant by "If ye are prepared, ye shall not fear." Anitra's expertise and preparedness plan has motivated and taught me what steps to take—she's made all the difference. I've gone from confusion about preparedness to actually being prepared!

—Gayla Dowdle

Can you say breath of fresh air? Every time I open my newly organized spice drawer I catch my breath because it is so inviting—alphabetized, uniform, and each lid is labeled. I know exactly what I have. It just feels good! And I find myself opening my pantry door just to stare at and enjoy the contents: labeled containers, neatly arranged shelves, matching jars, and boxes that hold it all. Even my kids keep the pantry cleaner because everything now has its place! Preparing foods just went from drudge to delight because it's all there—in its place and in my pantry!

—Martsie Webb

Anitra Kerr

I have a passion for self-reliance and self-improvement, because I believe that to be truly prepared for the uncertainties of tomorrow, we need to be living the principles of self-reliance every day. We need to be confident in who we are and how we can help ourselves and those we love. Becoming self-reliant must begin with an organized plan. It is a skill that should be practiced everyday, and must be tested over and over until one becomes master of that plan!

I learned this lesson at the age of ten, when my father was diagnosed with cancer. For nearly eighteen months he battled with this disease until he finally conquered it. Being self-employed, his income suffered as well. The thing that impressed me the most through that experience, however, was the peace of mind I felt, because my parents had prepared long before then for such an unexpected event. We were used to using our food storage and harvesting from our garden. My parents had saved money for such a rainy day as this one, and had not indulged in debt. So when we were compelled to be solely self-reliant, life still seemed to run normally—it was not a painful and stressful adjustment. Although we had a large family, my parents never had to ask for financial assistance, and there was always good nutritious food to eat. (Believe me, as a ten-year-old, food was always important!) I knew at an early age that I wanted to share this message of self-reliance with others, and that I wanted to provide this same kind of security for my own family one day.

Today I'm a wife, and the mother of four boys, and I am more excited than ever to share what I have learned with you. Over the last few years, I have had the opportunity to share my message with hundreds of people through classes, seminars, and my web site, www.simplylivingsmart.com. I have shown numerous people how to bring their food storage from the basement to the table and love it! I have taught individuals how to effectively organize not only their time, but their closets, their pantries, and their menu-planning. I have shared simple skills that empower individuals with the confidence they need to do more for themselves than they ever thought possible. Those who battle with picky eaters at home have learned my secrets for infusing more nutrition into meals their families already enjoy everyday. Others have found that they can free up many more hours in their week by simply following a routine and sticking to it. Many have been amazed at the organizational skills that I present in my book, and while those skills are so simple, people have found a method to their madness, and have turned their lives and those of their families into one of security and harmony.

Whether it's help with effective meal planning, plans for organizing, or just a little peace of mind that you're seeking, you'll love my book: *Simply Living Smart—Everyday Solutions for a More Organized You.*

Live Smart,

Live Simple,

Live Well!